WHAT IS IT

PHOTOS TO KEEP YOU GUESSING

by Ditz

WHAT IS IT?

Published in Great Britain and USA by
AAPPL Artists' and Photographers' Press Ltd.
10 Hillside   London SW19 4NH   UK
info@aappl.com   www.aappl.com

Sales and Distribution
UK and export: Turnaround Publisher Services Ltd.
orders@turnaround-uk.com
USA and Canada: Sterling Publishing Inc. NY
sales@sterlingpub.com

A catalogue record for this book is available from the British Library.

ISBN 1-904332-21-8 (hardback edition)

Art Director: Ditz   ditz@aappl.com
Design: Niki Nekuda   office@nekuda.at

Printed in China by Imago

What is it?

More than 200 photographs all
made to keep you guessing

it's the photographer in a bathroom
...but they won't all be this easy...

the shadow of pets playing in a sunny room

an old bird cage

an echinacea

a melon-baller

Terry's laughter lines

opposite page: cigarette smoke

making charcoal

a red poppy

opposite page: a seatbelt buckle on a plane

one used left boot

a cowboy's boot in the stirrup

a dog on his sofa

a pair of pinking-shears

a cowboy's lasso

opposite page: an old sweet chestnut

a rather large slug

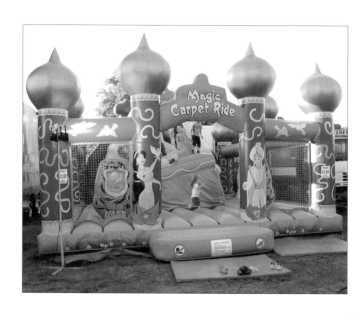

a dome on a bouncy castle

opposite page: a climbing wall

a hairdryer

opposite page: blackberries

opposite page: hamburgers on an open grill

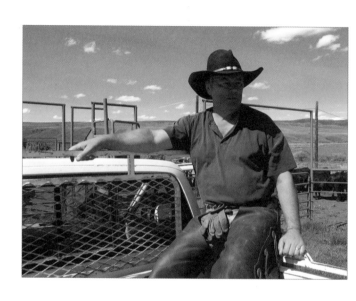

a protective grill on a ranch pick-up truck

opposite page: a heron

raindrops on a mountain ash

a roll of brown wrapping-paper

opposite page: the door of a washing machine

icicles

opposite page: a finial on a roof

a pair of kitchen scissors

opposite page: an outside staircase

opposite page: a tree-fungus

a cauliflower

opposite page: a very hairy ear

opposite page: a drummer

a colander

a phone

opposite page: frogspawn

the muzzle of a llama

opposite page: a lady's curly hair

a lamp in a motel bedroom

opposite page: a children's slide at a fair

opposite page: the Prince of Wales' polo shirt

ceiling lights in an amusement arcade

opposite page: a windmill

a boot-jack

opposite page: a telescope

bobbies at the fair

a lady up a ladder

opposite page: acorns

opposite page: the cat's whiskers

a tranquilising gun

a boy-eating tiger at a fair

opposite page: an antenna on a plane's wing

a toilet being flushed

a cowpat

opposite page: distortion through a tumbler

opposite page: a yellow poppy

a car windshield

a children's roundabout

opposite page: a lampshade

a champagne-bottle stopper

opposite page: an iron stove

opposite page: a flowerpot

a watering-can

a froglet

opposite page: a robin

an ornamental garden

a toadstool

a goat's skull

opposite page: a shot road sign

dirty jeans

an old home-made sledge

rose-hips

a goal

opposite page: a girl's hair

opposite page: a rocking-chair

measuring-spoons

the American flag

opposite page: a guitar player

opposite page: the guardsman's busby

lichen on a rock

opposite page: an eggwhisk

a rosebud

a bird-feeder

opposite page: a curious wooden bear

a horse's behind

a fan

a cloud at sunset

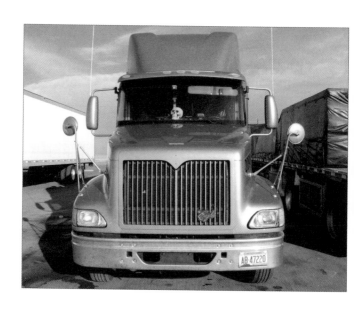

lights on a truck's roof

a fish slice

a hole-punch

opposite page: a very small, very red mushroom

the protective sheath on a cable

opposite page: hair-clips

a pair of scissors

a snail on a flowerpot

a pair of edible mushrooms

an old saloon

a stapler

opposite page: one soft roll...

...not what you thought...

opposite page: a roadsign

an upside-down snail

opposite page: a Canada goose

opposite page: a country road

spectacles in their case

reflections of dodgems at a fair

a computer-mouse

reflections in a pond

a tea-strainer

a tractor

a door-chain

opposite page: a pair of tassels

a foxglove

opposite page: a duck's calling card

a potato-masher

opposite page: snowy trees at night

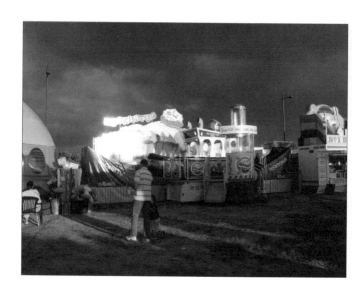

the roof of a fairground attraction

opposite page: the pickguard of a guitar

spectacles on their stand

opposite page: the cat's ear

opposite page: the robin's foot

a narrow-gauge railway trestle

a piglet

a belly button

the overflow in an old bathtub

opposite page: a cygnet

the shadow of horses and riders

an old broom

a whippet's mouth

making candyfloss

opposite page: insects on iris leaves

opposite page: an old bulrush

a cherry stoner/garlic press

an old lantern

duck's legs in a puddle

a desk lamp

living statues

opposite page: a melon

a concertina file

a book of matches

a swan

a pair of dressmaking-scissors

a helicopter

opposite page: a poly-tunnel

an ink bottle

an old cut log

Wiener schnitzel

a swallow's wings

opposite page: hoofprints in a rodeo arena

a plate of Mexican food

opposite page: red roses

a hot-air balloon

a wire coat-hanger

the photographer's brother

the step of an old steam-train

a decomposing leaf

a cowboy hat and truck

opposite page: a small moth on a lampshade

a cardboard box

opposite page: hungry caterpillars

a house on the move

opposite page: a letter-box

a dirty car-window

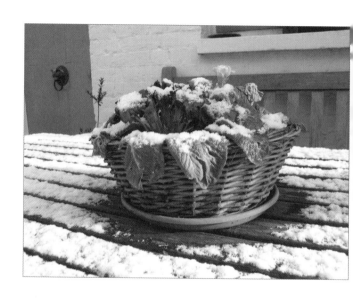

a garden table in winter

opposite page: a lemon

a neon sign

a doormat

lichen on a branch

opposite page: a coyote in the snow

a coconut

opposite page: a cheese-grater

an eroded hill

a fritillary

an old pick-up truck

a plug

algae in a stream

young fir-cones

opposite page: an ambulance at a horse show

a kitchen-towel

an apple-corer

opposite page: the door frame of house number 108 ½

opposite page: a one-man band

glasses in an old bar

a millrace

a roll of bubble-wrap

a dimmer switch

a silver birch

the raven's beak

street acrobats

kitchen foil

opposite page: a shaving-brush

a cupboard handle

an old fruit-press

distant rain at sunset

opposite page: a cobweb

opposite page: a cotton reel

young sweetcorn

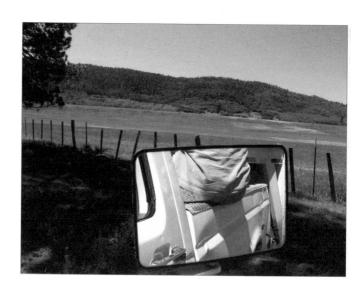

the image in the wing-mirror of a pick-up truck

the horse's mouth

a ceiling fan

oops!

a crow's skull

work on the design of this book

a cat's toes

a thousand thanks to Niki

who made the book look just like I thought it should

Dik